Oskar Schindler

Terry Barber

ACTS OF
COURAGE
SERIES

Oskar Schindler is published by
Grass Roots Press, a division of Literacy Services of Canada Ltd.

PHONE 1–888–303–3213
WEBSITE www.grassrootsbooks.net

ACKNOWLEDGMENTS

We acknowledge the financial support of the Government of Canada through the Book Publishing Industry Development Program (BPIDP) for our publishing activities.

We acknowledge the support of
the Alberta Foundation for the Arts
for our publishing programs.

Editors: Dr. Pat Campbell and Linda Kita-Bradley
Image research: Dr. Pat Campbell
Book design: Lara Minja, Lime Design Inc.

Library and Archives Canada Cataloguing in Publication

Barber, Terry, date
    Oskar Schindler / Terry Barber.

ISBN 978-1-894593-85-4

    1. Schindler, Oskar, 1908-1974. 2. World War, 1939-1945—Jews—Rescue. 3. Holocaust, Jewish (1939-1945) 4. Righteous Gentiles in the Holocaust—Biography. 5. Readers for new literates. I. Title.

PE1126.N43B36643 2008   428.6'2   C2008-901984-9

Printed in Canada

Contents

Hitler becomes Germany's leader on January 30, 1933.

Adolf Hitler salutes a crowd of people.

The Nazis' Rise to Power

In 1933, the **Nazi Party** gains control of Germany. Hitler is the leader of the Nazi Party. Germany is in a bad way. Germany has lost World War I. Hitler blames the Jews for this loss. Hitler blames the Jews for Germany's problems.

Germany suffers from the **Great Depression** of the 1930s.

This German sign says, "Jews are not welcomed here."

The Holocaust

The Nazis want the Jews to leave
Germany. The Nazis pass laws that
make life hard for Jews. Jews cannot
own property. Jews cannot own a
business. Their children cannot go to
school. By 1939, the Jews do not have
any rights.

Jews must carry
identity cards.

The Germans **invade** Poland on September 1, 1939.

The Holocaust

Germany starts World War II in 1939.
The Nazis control most of Europe.
Life becomes worse for the Jews. The
Nazis move the Jews to **ghettos**. The
ghettos are dirty and crowded. Many
Jews die from hunger and sickness.

These children
beg for food
in a ghetto.

Jewish men work at a shoe factory.

Many Jews are forced to work 14 to 16 hours a day.

The Holocaust

The Nazis treat the Jews like slaves.
They send many Jews to labour
camps. Many of the Jews work in
factories. They are not paid for their
work. Some are beaten to death. Some
are worked to death.

Jewish women work at a labour camp.

The
Nazis also
kill other groups,
including Gypsies
and Poles.

This entrance leads to the
Auschwitz death camp.

The Holocaust

The Nazis have a plan. This plan is called the **Final Solution**. They want to kill all the Jews in Europe. The Nazis begin to build **death camps** in 1941. Jews are sent to the camps in trains.

The bodies of Jews in the Auschwitz death camp.

In 1939, Oskar moves to Krakow, Poland.

Schindler's Business

Oskar Schindler is a Nazi. He moves to Poland in 1939. He wants to **profit** from the war. He opens a factory. His factory makes pots and pans. His factory also makes **shells**. The Nazis need shells for the war.

Oskar is born in 1908. His parents are German.

Oskar sings at a dinner party.

Schindler's Business

Oskar loves the good things in life. He is married. But, he still loves other women. He loves wealth. He loves whiskey. Women, wealth, and whiskey. The three "Ws" are big in Oskar's life.

Oskar marries Emilie Pelzl on March 6, 1928.

These workers stand in front of Oskar's factory.

Schindler's Business

Many Jews work in Oskar's factory. Oskar is good to his Jewish workers. He feeds the workers. He protects them from the Nazis. The workers feel safe with Oskar. They work hard for him.

Oskar does not make his Jews work long hours.

Oskar hires men, women, and children.

Schindler's Business

Most factory owners hire strong, healthy Jews. Oskar is different. Oskar hires old workers. Oskar hires sick workers. Oskar hires women and children. He protects every Jew who works in his factory.

A German tells his two dogs to attack a Jewish man.

Schindler's Vows

At night, the Jewish workers return to the ghetto. One day, Oskar sees the Nazis **raid** a Jewish ghetto. They shoot the Jews. The Nazis' dogs attack the Jews. Oskar feels sick. His workers live in that ghetto.

The Nazis kill about 6 million Jews during World War II.

Oskar stands in front of his factory.

Schindler's Vows

Oskar **vows** to save his workers. He decides to build a camp by his factory. His workers will live in this camp. They will be safe. The Nazis do not like this idea. Oskar **bribes** the Nazis. They let Oskar build the camp.

The camp opens in 1943.

Oskar enjoys himself at a dinner party
with German officers.

Schindler's Vows

Oskar makes a second vow. He will not help the Nazis win the war. Oskar will just pretend to help the Nazis. He pretends to be their friend. He holds parties for the Nazis. He drinks with the Nazis. He lies to the Nazis.

Oskar's factory

Schindler's Plan

It is 1944. Germany is losing the war.
The **Allies** are getting close to Poland.
The Germans tell Oskar to shut down
his factory. The Nazis plan to send
his workers to a labour camp. Oskar
makes a plan to save his workers.

The Allies include Great Britain, the Commonwealth, France, the Soviet Union, the U.S., and China.

29

Oskar is born in Svitavy, Czechoslovakia.

Poland

Sudetenland

Svitavy ★

Brunnlitz ★

Czechoslovakia

Austria

Hungary

Oskar builds his factory in Brunnlitz.

Schindler's Plan

Oskar decides to buy a factory in his homeland. He wants to take his Jewish workers with him. Oskar must get the Nazis to agree. Oskar bribes the Nazis again. The Nazis agree.

Oskar's homeland is Czechoslovakia.

z.Zt. 3591 Emdenau, den 24.8.64
Sanatorium Stein

Sehr geehrter H...

KL Groß – Rosen – AL Brünnlitz / Häftl.-Liste (Männer) 18.4.45-Blatt 7

Lfd. Nr.	H.Art u.Nam.	H.Nr.	Name und Vorname	Geburts- datum	Beruf
361	Ju.Po.	69208	Hahn Dawid	20.10.97	Werkzeugschlosser
362	" "	9	Immerglück Zygmunt	13.6. 24	Stanzer
363	" "	1o	Katz Isaak Josef	3.12.08	Klempnergehilfe
364	" "	1	Wiener Samuel	11. 5.o7	Tischlergehilfe
365	" "	2	Rosner Leopold	26, 6.08	Maler
366	" "	3	Gewelbe Jakob	22. 9.97	Photografmeister
367	" "	4	Korn Edmund	7. 4.12	Metallarbeiter
368	" "	5	Penner Jonas	2. 2.15	Stanzer
369	" "	6	Wachtel Roman	5.11.05	Industriediamanten
37o	" "	7	Immerglück Mendel	24.9.03	Eisendrehergeselle
371	" "	8	Wichter Feiwel	25. 7.26	Metallverarbeite
372	" "	9	Landschaft Aron	7. 7.09	" "
373	" "	6922o	Wandersmann Markus	14. 9.06	Stanzer
374	" "	1	Rosenthal Izrael	24.1o.09	Schreibkraft
375	" "	2	Silberschlag Hersch	7. 4.12	Ang.Metallverarbeite
376	" "	3	Liban Jan	29. 4.24	Wasserinst.Gehilfe
377	" "	4	Kohane Chiel	15. 9. 25	Zimmerer
378	" "	5	Senftmann Dawid	6. 9.09	Ang.Metallverarbeite
379	" "	6	Kupferberg Izrael	4. 9.98	Schlossermeister
38o	" "	7	Buchführer Norbert	12. 6.22	Lackierer Geselle
381	" "	8	Horowitz Schachne	3.1288	Schriftsetzermei.ste
382	" "	9	Segal Richard	9.11.23	Steinbruchmineur
383	" "	6925o	Jakubowicz Dawid	15. 4.26	"
384	" "	1	Sommer Josef	21.12.14	ang.Metallverarb.
385	" "	2	Smolars Szymon	15. 4.04	"
386	" "	3	Rechem Ryszard	3o. 5.21	"
387	" "	4	Szlamowicz Chaim	16. 5.24	Automechank.Gs.
388	" "	5	Kleinberg Szaija	1. 4.2o	Stanzer
389	" "	6	Miedziuch Michael	3.11.16	Steinbruchmineur
39o	+ "	7	Millmann Bernhard	24.12.15	Fleischergeselle
391	" "	8	Königl Marek	2.11.11.	Stanzer
392	" "	9	Jakubowicz Chaim	1o. 1.19	Ang.Mettallverarb.
393	" "	6924o	Domb Izrael	23. 1.08	Steinbruchmineur
394	" "	1	Klimburt Abram	1.11.13	Schreibkraft
395	" "	2	Wisniak Abram	3o	Koch
396	" "	3	Schreiber Leopold	15.1o.25	Lehrling
397	" "	4	Silberstein Kacob	1. 1.oo	Schlossergeselle
398	" "	5	Eidner Pinkus	2o.12.14	Galvanisourmeister
399	" "	6	Goldberg Perisch	17. 5.13	Dampfkesselheizer
4oo	" "	7	Feiner Josef	16. 5.15	ang.Metallverarb.
4o1	" "	8	Feiner Wilhelm	21.1o.17	Automechanikcer
4o2	" "	9	Löw Zoycze	28. 6.97	Stanzer
4o3	" "	6925o	Löw Jacob	3. 3.oo	Kesselschmied Meist.
4o4	" "	1	Pozniak Szloma	15. 9.16	"
4o5	" "	2	Ratz Wolf	2o. 6.09	Bäcker
4o6	" "	3	Lewkowicz Ferdinand	12. 3.09	Metallverarb.
4o7	" "	4	Lax Ryszard	9. 7.24	Arzt Chrirug
4o8	" "	5	Semmel Berek	5. 1.o5	Automechaniker Ges.
4o9	" "	6	Horowitz Isidor	25. 9.95	Tischler Gehilfe
41o	" "	7	Meisels Szlama	2.2.16	ang.Installateur
411	" "	8	Kormann Abraham	15. 1. o9	Fleischergeselle
412	" "	9	Joachimsmann Abraham	19.12.95	Buchhalter
413	" "	6926o	Sawicki Samuel	9. 4.17	Stanzer
414	" "	1	Rosner Wilhelm	14. 9.25	Koch
415	" "	2	Hirschberg Symon	23. 7.08	Schlossergehilfe
416	" "	3	Goldberg Bernhard	1o.1o.16	Stanzer
417	" "	4	Gerstner Leib	16.1o.12	Koch
418	" "	5	Hudes Naftali	1o. 7.99	Glaser
		6	Pufeles Maureycy	5.1o.12	Bilanzbuchhalter
			Wulkan Markus	31.1o.1o	Bronz-Silberschmied

Schindler's list of 1,200 Polish Jews.

Schindler's List

Oskar prepares to move his workers. He starts to make a list of names. Other Jews hear about the list. They want their names on the list, too. The final list has 1,200 names. It is called Schindler's List.

The trains are very crowded.

Schindler's List

The new factory is far away.
The 1,200 Jews travel in box cars.
The Nazis make the Jews stop at
death camps. Men and women go to
different death camps. Oskar bribes
the Nazis to release his workers.
The Nazis let them go.

A Jewish woman eats a bowl of soup.

Schindler's Factory

The Jews arrive at Oskar's new factory. They are tired and hungry. Oskar greets the workers. He feeds them hot soup. Oskar tells the Jews he will take care of them. The Jews feel safe with Oskar.

A man holds some shells.

Schindler's Factory

Oskar's workers make shells for the war. This keeps the Nazis happy. The Nazis do not check the shells. The Nazis do not know that the shells will not work. Oskar risks his life to make shells that do not work.

The Allies free these Jews.

After the War

World War II ends in 1945. The Jews are free. But, Oskar must hide from the Nazis and the Allies. The Nazis call him a Jew-lover. The Allies call him a war criminal.

Oskar and his wife have no money. Jewish groups help to support them.

Hitler kills himself on April 30, 1945.

Oskar and Emilie in Argentina.

After the War

Oskar and his wife move to Argentina
in 1949. He tries to make money as a
farmer. He fails. Oskar is not happy.
Oskar leaves his wife and moves back
to Germany. He lives a lonely life.

Oskar drives a tractor on his farm.

Oskar Schindler's grave.

After the War

Oskar dies in Germany in 1974. He is 66 years old. Oscar is buried in Israel. Many of his Jewish workers go to the funeral. They weep for the man who saved them. Oskar's act of courage saved many Jews.

Glossary

Allies: nations that fought against Germany and other central powers in World War II.

bribe: something given to a person in exchange for a favour.

death camp: a place built by the Nazis to kill Jews.

Final Solution: code-name for the Nazi's plan to murder all the Jews in Europe.

ghetto: a street or city section where only Jews lived.

Great Depression: a time of high unemployment, falling stock prices, and low wages.

Holocaust: persecution and murder of about 6 million Jews in Europe by the Nazis.

invade: to enter by force to conquer.

Nazi Party: the racist and anti-Semitic German political party founded on January 5, 1919.

profit: to gain or benefit.

raid: a sudden attack.

shell: the metal case that holds the object fired from a gun.

vow: a promise.

Talking About the Book

What did you learn about Oskar Schindler?

What did you learn about the Holocaust?

What lessons can the world learn from the Holocaust?

Why do you think Oskar helped the Jews survive?

Describe Oskar's act of courage.

Why do you think Oskar Schindler was buried in Israel?

Picture Credits

Front cover: © United States Holocaust Memorial Museum. Contents page (top right): © Yad Vashem; (bottom): © USHMM. Page 4: © USHMM. Pages 6 – 7: © USHMM. Page 8: © Bettmann/CORBIS. Pages 9 - 13. © USHMM. Page 14: © Andreas (Andy) N Korsos, Professional Cartographer, Arcturus Consulting. Pages 16 - 28: © USHMM. Page 30: Andreas (Andy) N Korsos, Professional Cartographer, Arcturus Consulting. Page 32: © Reuters/CORBIS. Pages 34 - 36: © USHMM. Page 38: © Michael Freeman/CORBIS. Page 40: © USHMM. Pages 42-43: © Yad Vashem. Page 44: © Ddanzig/flickr.